Advanced Machine Learning

Mastering Level Learning with Python

Contents

Chapter 1: Introduction

1.1 What is Advanced Machine Learning

Ongoing advances in computational power (per Moore's Law) have begun to make machine learning, once mostly a research discipline, more viable in commercial contexts. This has caused an explosion of new applications and new or rediscovered techniques, catapulting the obscure concepts of data science, AI, and machine learning into the public consciousness and strategic planning of companies internationally.

The rapid development of machine learning applications is fueled by an ongoing struggle to continually innovate, playing out at an array of research labs. The techniques developed by these pioneers are seeding new application areas and experiencing growing public awareness. While some of the innovations sought in AI and applied machine learning are still elusively far from readiness, others are a reality. Self-driving cars, sophisticated image recognition and altering capability, ever-greater strides in genetics research, and perhaps most pervasively of all, increasingly tailored content in our digital stores, e-mail inboxes, and online lives.

With all of these possibilities and more at the fingertips of the committed data scientist, the profession is seeing a meteoric, if clumsy, growth. Not only are there far more data scientists and AI practitioners now than there were even two years ago (in early 2014), but the accessibility and openness around solutions at the high end of machine learning research has increased.

Research teams at Google and Facebook began to share

more and more of their architecture, languages, models, and tools in the hope of seeing them applied and improved on by the growing data scientist population.

The machine learning community matured enough to begin seeing trends as popular algorithms were defined or rediscovered. To put this more accurately, pre-existing trends from a mainly research community began to receive great attention from industry, with one product being a group of machine learning experts straddling industry and academia. Another product, the subject of this section, is a growing awareness of advanced algorithms that can be used to crack the frontier problems of the current day. From month to month, we see new advances made, scores rise, and the frontier moves ever further out.

What all of this means is that there may never have been a better time to move into the field of data science and develop your machine learning skillset. The introductory algorithms (including clustering, regression models, and neural network architectures) and tools are widely covered in web courses and blog content. While the techniques at the cutting edge of data science (including deep learning, semi-supervised algorithms, and ensembles) remain less accessible, the techniques themselves are now available through software libraries in multiple languages. All that's needed is the combination of theoretical knowledge and practical guidance to implement models correctly. That is the requirement that this book was written to address.

1.2 Prerequisite

You should have extensive knowledge about Python/R, algorithms and techniques of Machine Learning. (See Beginner's Guide to Machine & Intermediate's Guide to Machine Learning).

1.3 Recap of Intermediate's Guide to Machine Learning

Learning means the acquisition of knowledge or skills through study or experience. Based on this, we can define machine learning (ML) as follows −

It may be defined as the field of computer science, more specifically an application of artificial intelligence, which provides computer systems the ability to learn with data and improve from experience without being explicitly programmed.

Basically, the main focus of machine learning is to allow the computers learn automatically without human intervention. Now the question arises that how such learning can be started and done? It can be started with the observations of data. The data can be some examples, instruction or some direct experiences too. Then on the basis of this input, machine makes better decision by looking for some patterns in data.

Machine Learning Algorithms helps computer system learn without being explicitly programmed. These algorithms are categorized into supervised or unsupervised.

- Supervised Machine Learning
- Unsupervised Machine Learning
- Reinforcement Machine Learning

Mainly supervised leaning problems can be divided into the following two kinds of problems –

- **Classification** – A problem is called classification problem when we have the categorized output such as "black", "teaching", "non-teaching", etc.

- **Regression** – A problem is called regression problem when we have the real value output such as "distance", "kilogram", etc.

Decision tree, random forest, KNN, logistic regression are the examples of supervised machine learning algorithms.

Unsupervised learning problems can be divided into the following two kinds of problem –

- **Clustering** – In clustering problems, we need to discover the inherent groupings in the data. For example, grouping customers by their purchasing behavior.
- **Association** – A problem is called association problem because such kinds of problem require discovering the rules that describe large portions of our data. For example, finding the customers who buy both **x** and **y**.

K-means for clustering, Apriori algorithm for association are the examples of unsupervised machine learning algorithms.

1.3.1 Regression

Regression techniques are one of the most popular statistical techniques used for predictive modeling and data mining tasks. On average, analytics professionals know only 2-3 types of regression which are commonly used in real world. They are linear and logistic regression. But the fact is there are more than 10 types of regression algorithms designed for various types of analysis. Each type has its own significance. Every analyst must know which form of regression to use depending on type of data and distribution.

1.3.2 Classification

In machine learning and statistics, classification is a supervised learning approach in which the computer program learns from the data input given to it and then uses this learning to classify new observation. This data set may simply be bi-class (like identifying whether the person is male or female or that the mail is spam or non-spam) or it may be multi-class too. Some examples of classification problems are: speech recognition, handwriting recognition, bio metric identification, document classification etc.

Classification can be performed on structured or unstructured data. Classification is a technique where we categorize data into a given number of classes. The main goal of a classification problem is to identify the category/class to which a new data will fall under.

1.3.3 Clustering

Clustering is the task of dividing the population or data points into a number of groups such that data points in the same groups are more similar to other data points in the same group and dissimilar to the data points in other groups. It is basically a collection of objects on the basis of similarity and dissimilarity between them. Clustering is very much important as it determines the intrinsic grouping among the unlabeled data present. There are no criteria for a good clustering. It depends on the user, what is the criteria they may use which satisfy their need. For instance, we could be interested in finding representatives for homogeneous groups (data reduction), in finding "natural clusters" and describe their unknown properties ("natural" data types), in finding useful and suitable groupings ("useful" data classes) or in finding unusual data objects (outlier detection). This algorithm must make some assumptions which constitute the similarity of points and each assumption make different and equally valid clusters.

Clustering is very much important as it determines the intrinsic grouping among the unlabeled data present. There are no criteria for a good clustering. It depends on the user, what is the criteria they may use which satisfy their need. For instance, we could be interested in finding representatives for homogeneous groups (data reduction), in finding "natural clusters" and describe their unknown properties ("natural" data types), in finding useful and suitable groupings ("useful" data classes) or in finding unusual data objects (outlier detection). This algorithm must make some assumptions which constitute the similarity of points and each assumption make different and equally valid clusters.

1.3.4 Natural Language Processing

Humans have been writing things down for thousands of years. Over that time, our brain has gained a tremendous amount of experience in understanding natural language. When we read something written on a piece of paper or in a blog post on the internet, we understand what that thing really means in the real-world. We feel the emotions that reading that thing elicits and we often visualize how that thing would look in real life.

Natural Language Processing (NLP) is a sub-field of Artificial Intelligence that is focused on enabling computers to understand and process human languages, to get computers closer to a human-level understanding of language. Computers don't yet have the same intuitive understanding of natural language that humans do. They can't really understand what the language is really trying to say. In a nutshell, a computer can't read between the lines.

NLP is a way for computers to analyze, understand, and derive meaning from human language in a smart and useful way. By utilizing NLP, developers can organize and structure knowledge to perform tasks such as automatic summarization, translation, named entity recognition, relationship extraction, sentiment analysis, speech recognition, and topic segmentation.

Natural Language Processing (NLP) is a sub-field of Artificial Intelligence that is focused on enabling computers to understand and process human languages, to get computers closer to a human-level understanding of language. Computers don't yet have the same intuitive understanding of natural language that humans do. They can't really understand what the language is really trying to say. In a nutshell, a computer can't read between the lines.

NLP is a way for computers to analyze, understand, and derive meaning from human language in a smart and useful way. By utilizing NLP, developers can organize and structure knowledge to perform tasks such as automatic summarization, translation, named entity recognition, relationship extraction, sentiment analysis, speech recognition, and topic segmentation.

That being said, recent advances in Machine Learning (ML) have enabled computers to do quite a lot of useful things with natural language! Deep Learning has enabled us to write programs to perform things like language translation, semantic understanding, and text summarization. All of these things add real-world value, making it easy for you to understand and perform computations on large blocks of text without the manual effort.

The development of NLP has its meaning because of some specific problems and phenomena that arrive when we study natural language. Most of the times, these problems are unique in comparison to the problems that emerge in other fields of computer science or engineering, and that is in part what makes NLP such an interesting and different area.

1.3.5 Reinforcement Learning

This type of learning is used to reinforce or strengthen the network based on critic information. That is, a network being trained under reinforcement learning, receives some feedback from the environment. However, the feedback is evaluative and not instructive as in the case of supervised learning. Based on this feedback, the network performs the adjustments of the weights to obtain better critic information in future.

Reinforcement learning is an approach to machine learning that is inspired by behaviorist psychology. It is similar to how a child learns to perform a new task. Reinforcement learning contrasts with other machine learning approaches in that the algorithm is not explicitly told how to perform a task, but works through the problem on its own.

As an agent, which could be a self-driving car or a program playing chess, interacts with its environment, receives a reward state depending on how it performs, such as driving to destination safely or winning a game. Conversely, the agent receives a penalty for performing incorrectly, such as going off the road or being checkmated.

The agent over time makes decisions to maximize its reward and minimize its penalty using dynamic programming. The advantage of this approach to artificial intelligence is that it allows an AI program to learn without a programmer spelling out how an agent should perform the task.

This learning process is similar to supervised learning but we might have very less information.

Now we will further discuss advanced topics of Machine Learning.

Let's get started!

Chapter 2: Unsupervised Machine Learning

2.1 Introduction

In this chapter, you will learn how to apply unsupervised learning techniques to identify patterns and structure within datasets.

Unsupervised learning techniques are a valuable set of tools for exploratory analysis. They bring out patterns and structure within datasets, which yield information that may be informative in itself or serve as a guide to further analysis. It's critical to

have a solid set of unsupervised learning tools that you can apply to help break up unfamiliar or complex datasets into actionable information.

We'll begin by reviewing Principal Component Analysis (PCA), a fundamental data manipulation technique with a range of dimensionality reduction applications. Next, we will discuss k-means clustering, a widely-used and approachable unsupervised learning technique. Then, we will discuss Kohenen's Self-Organizing Map (SOM), a method of topological clustering that enables the projection of complex datasets into two dimensions.

Throughout the chapter, we will spend some time discussing how to effectively   apply these techniques to make high-dimensional datasets readily accessible. We will use the UCI Handwritten Digits dataset to demonstrate technical applications   of each algorithm. In the course of discussing and applying each technique, we will review practical applications and methodological questions, particularly regarding how to calibrate and validate each technique as well as which performance measures are valid. To recap, then, we will be covering the following topics in order:

- Principal component analysis
- k-means clustering
- Self-organizing maps

2.2 Principal Component Analysis

In order to work effectively with high-dimensional datasets, it is important to have a set of techniques that can reduce this dimensionality down to manageable levels. The advantages of this dimensionality reduction include the ability to plot multivariate data in two dimensions, capture the majority of a dataset's informational content within a minimal number of features, and, in some contexts, identify collinear model components.

Probably the most widely-used dimensionality reduction technique today is PCA. As we'll be applying PCA in multiple contexts throughout this book, it's appropriate for us to review the technique, understand the theory behind it, and write Python code to effectively apply it.

2.2.1 PCA- A Primer

PCA is a powerful decomposition technique; it allows one to break down a highly multivariate dataset into a set of orthogonal components. When taken together in sufficient number, these components can explain almost all of the dataset's variance. In essence, these components deliver an abbreviated description of the dataset. PCA has a broad set of applications and its extensive utility makes it well worth our time to cover.

PCA works by successively identifying the axis of greatest variance in a dataset (the principal components). It does this as follows:

- Identifying the center point of the dataset.
- Calculating the covariance matrix of the data.
- Calculating the eigenvectors of the covariance matrix.
- Orthonormalizing the eigenvectors.
- Calculating the proportion of variance represented by each eigenvector.

Let's unpack these concepts briefly:

- **Covariance** is effectively variance applied to multiple dimensions; it is the variance between two or more variables. While a single value can capture the variance in one dimension or variable, it is necessary to use a *2 x 2* matrix to capture the covariance between two variables, a *3 x 3* matrix to capture the covariance between three variables, and so on. So the first step in PCA is to calculate this covariance matrix.

- An **Eigenvector** is a vector that is specific to a dataset and linear transformation. Specifically, it is the vector that does not change in direction before and after the transformation is performed. To get a better feeling for how this works, imagine that you're holding a rubber band, straight, between both hands. Let's say you stretch the band out until it is taut between your hands. The eigenvector is the vector that did not change direction between before the stretch and during it; in this case, it's the vector running directly through the center of the band from one hand to the other.

- **Orthogonalization** is the process of finding two vectors that are orthogonal (at right angles) to one another. In an n-dimensional data space, the process of orthogonalization takes a set of vectors and yields a set of orthogonal vectors.

- **Orthonormalization** is an orthogonalization process that also normalizes the product.

- **Eigenvalue** (roughly corresponding to the length of the eigenvector) is used to calculate the proportion of variance represented by each eigenvector. This is done by dividing the eigenvalue for each eigenvector by the sum of eigenvalues for all eigenvectors.

2.3 Introducing K-means Clustering

In the previous section, you learned that unsupervised machine learning algorithms are used to extract key structural or information content from large, possibly complex datasets. These algorithms do so with little or no manual input and function without the need for training data (sets of labeled explanatory and response variables needed to train an algorithm in order to recognize the desired classification boundaries). This means that unsupervised algorithms are effective tools to generate information about the structure and content of new or unfamiliar datasets. They allow the analyst to build a strong understanding in a fraction of the time.

2.3.1 Clustering- A primer

Clustering is probably the archetypal unsupervised learning technique for several reasons.

A lot of development time has been sunk into optimizing clustering algorithms, with

efficient implementations available in most data science languages including Python.

Clustering algorithms tend to be very fast, with smoothed implementations running in polynomial time. This makes it uncomplicated to run multiple clustering configurations, even over large datasets. Scalable clustering implementations also exist that parallelize the algorithm to run over TB-scale datasets.

Clustering algorithms are frequently easily understood and their operation is thus easy to explain if necessary.

The most popular clustering algorithm is k-means; this algorithm forms k-many clusters by first randomly initiating the clusters as k-many points in the data space. Each of these points is the mean of a cluster. An iterative process then occurs, running as follows:

Each point is assigned to a cluster based on the least (within cluster) sum of squares, which is intuitively the nearest mean.

The center (centroid) of each cluster becomes the new mean. This causes each of the means to shift.

Over enough iterations, the centroids move into positions that minimize a performance metric (the performance metric most commonly used is the "within cluster least sum of squares" measure). Once this measure is minimized, observations are no longer reassigned during iteration; at this point the algorithm has converged on a solution.

Helpfully, scikit-learn uses the k-means++ algorithm by default, which improves over the original k-means algorithm in terms of both running time and success rate in avoiding poor clustering.

The algorithm achieves this by running an initialization procedure to find cluster centroids that approximate minimal variance within classes.

You may have spotted from the preceding code that we're using a set of performance estimators to track how well our k-means application is performing. It isn't practical to measure the performance of a clustering algorithm based on a single correctness percentage or using the same performance measures that are commonly used with other algorithms. The definition of success for clustering algorithms is that they provide an interpretation of how input data is grouped that trades off between several factors, including class separation, in-group similarity, and cross-group difference.

The homogeneity score is a simple, zero-to-one-bounded measure of the degree to which clusters contain only assignments of a given class. A score of one indicates that all clusters contain measurements from a single class. This measure is complimented by the completeness score, which is a similarly bounded measure of the extent

to which all members of a given class are assigned to the same cluster. As such, a completeness score and homogeneity score of one indicates a perfect clustering solution.

The validity measure (v-measure) is a harmonic mean of the homogeneity and completeness scores, which is exactly analogous to the F-measure for binary classification. In essence, it provides a single, 0-1-scaled value to monitor both homogeneity and completeness.

The Adjusted Rand Index (ARI) is a similarity measure that tracks the consensus between sets of assignments. As applied to clustering, it measures the consensus between the true, pre-existing observation labels and the labels predicted as an output of the clustering algorithm. The Rand index measures labeling similarity on a 0-1 bound scale, with one equaling perfect prediction labels.

The main challenge with all of the preceding performance measures as well as other similar measures (for example, Akaike's mutual information criterion) is that they require an understanding of the ground truth, that is, they require some or all of the data under inspection to be labeled. If labels do not exist and cannot be generated, these measures won't work. In practice, this is a pretty substantial drawback as very few datasets come prelabeled and the creation of labels can be time-consuming.

2.4 Self Organizing Maps

A SOM is a technique to generate topological representations of data in reduced dimensions. It is one of a number of techniques with such applications, with a better-known alternative being PCA. However, SOMs present unique opportunities, both as dimensionality reduction techniques and as a visualization format.

2.4.1 SOM-A Primer

The SOM algorithm involves iteration over many simple operations. When applied at a smaller scale, it behaves similarly to k-means clustering (as we'll see shortly). At a larger scale, SOMs reveal the topology of complex datasets in a powerful way.

A SOM is made up of a grid (commonly rectangular or hexagonal) of nodes, where each node contains a weight vector that is of the same dimensionality as the input dataset. The nodes may be initialized randomly, but an initialization that roughly approximates the distribution of the dataset will tend to train faster.

The algorithm iterates as observations are presented as input. Iteration takes the following form:

Identifying the winning node in the current configuration—the Best Matching Unit (BMU). The BMU is identified by measuring the Euclidean distance in the data space of all the weight vectors.

The BMU is adjusted (moved) towards the input vector. Neighboring nodes are also adjusted, usually by lesser amounts, with the magnitude of neighboring movement being dictated by a neighborhood function. (Neighborhood functions vary. In this chapter, we'll use a Gaussian neighborhood function.)

This process repeats over potentially many iterations, using sampling if appropriate, until the network converges (reaching a position where presenting a new input does not provide an opportunity to minimize loss).

A node in a SOM is not unlike that of a neural network. It typically possesses a weight vector of length equal to the dimensionality of the input dataset. This means that the topology of the input dataset can be preserved and visualized through a lower-dimensional mapping.

The code for this SOM class implementation is available in the book repository in the som.py script. For now, let's start working with the SOM algorithm in a familiar context.

We started out by applying PCA, a widely-utilized dimensionality reduction technique, to help us understand and visualize a high-dimensional dataset. We then followed up by clustering the data using k-means clustering, identifying means of improving and measuring our k-means analysis through performance metrics, the elbow method, and cross-validation. We found that k-means on the digits dataset, taken as is, didn't deliver exceptional results. This was due to class overlap that we spotted through PCA. We overcame this weakness by applying PCA as a preprocess to improve our subsequent clustering results.

Finally, we developed a SOM algorithm that delivered a cleaner separation of the digit classes than PCA.

Having learned some key basics around unsupervised learning techniques and analytical methodology, let's dive into the use of some more powerful unsupervised learning algorithms.

Chapter 3: ANN & CNN

3.1 Artificial Neural Networks (ANN)

The term 'neural network' has its origins in attempts to find mathematical representations of information processing in biological systems (McCulloch and Pitts, 1943; Widrow and Hoff, 1960; Rosenblatt, 1962; Rumelhart et al., 1986). Indeed, it has been used very broadly to cover a wide range of different models, many of which have been the subject of exaggerated claims regarding their biological plausibility. From the perspective of practical applications of pattern recognition, however,

biological realism would impose entirely unnecessary constraints. Our focus in this chapter is therefore on neural networks as efficient models for statistical pattern recognition. In particular, we shall restrict our attention to the specific class of neural networks that have proven to be of greatest practical value, namely the multilayer perceptron. We begin by considering the functional form of the network model, including the specific parameterization of the basic functions, and we then discuss the problem of determining the network parameters within a maximum likelihood framework, which involves the solution of a nonlinear optimization problem. This requires the evaluation of derivatives of the log likelihood function with respect to the network parameters, and we shall see how these can be obtained efficiently using the technique of error backpropagation. We shall also show how the backpropagation framework can be extended to allow other derivatives to be evaluated, such as the Jacobian and Hessian matrices.

In information technology (IT), a neural network is a system of hardware and/or software patterned after the operation of neurons in the human brain. Neural networks -- also called artificial neural networks -- are a variety of deep learning technology, which also falls under the umbrella of artificial intelligence, or AI.

Commercial applications of these technologies generally focus on solving complex signal processing or pattern recognition problems. Examples of significant commercial applications since 2000 include handwriting recognition for check processing, speech-to-text transcription, oil-exploration data analysis, weather prediction and facial recognition.

3.1.1 Pattern Recognition

Pattern recognition is the ability to detect arrangements of characteristics or data that yield information about a given system or data set. In a technological context, a pattern might be recurring sequences of data over time that can be used to predict trends, particular configurations of features in images that identify objects, frequent combinations of words and phrases for natural language processing (NLP), or particular clusters of behavior on a network that could indicate an attack -- among almost endless other possibilities.

Pattern recognition is essential to many overlapping areas of IT, including big data analytics, biometric identification, security and artificial intelligence (AI).

Some examples of pattern recognition:

Facial recognition software takes in data related to the characteristics of a person's face and uses an algorithm to match that specific pattern to an individual record in a database.

Pattern recognition algorithms in meteorological software can detect recurring connections among weather data that can be used to forecast probable future weather events.

Network intrusion detection (NID) software rules describe patterns of behaviors and events that can indicate illegitimate traffic.

In 1997, IBM's Deep Blue used its ability to recognize patterns of play to defeat world chess champion Garry Kasparov.

In the context of AI, pattern recognition is a sub-category of machine learning (ML).

3.1.2 How Artificial Neural Networks Work

A neural network usually involves a large number of processors operating in parallel and arranged in tiers. The first tier receives the raw input information -- analogous to optic nerves in human visual processing. Each successive tier receives the output from the tier preceding it, rather than from the raw input -- in the same way neurons further from the optic nerve receive signals from those closer to it. The last tier produces the output of the system.

Each processing node has its own small sphere of knowledge, including what it has seen and any rules it was originally programmed with or developed for itself. The tiers are highly interconnected, which means each node in tier n will be connected to many nodes in tier n-1-- its inputs -- and in tier n+1, which provides input for those nodes. There may be one or multiple nodes in the output layer, from which the answer it produces can be read.

Neural networks are notable for being adaptive, which means they modify themselves as they learn from initial training and subsequent runs provide more information about the world. The most basic learning model is centered on weighting the input streams, which is how each node weights the importance of input from each of its predecessors. Inputs that contribute to getting right answers are weighted higher.

3.1.3 How Neural Networks Learn

Typically, a neural network is initially trained or fed large amounts of data. Training consists of providing input and telling the network what the output should be. For example, to build a network to identify the faces of actors, initial training might be a series of pictures of actors, non-actors, masks, statuary, animal faces and so on. Each input is accompanied by the matching identification, such as actors' names, "not actor" or "not human" information. Providing the answers allows the model to adjust its internal weightings to learn how to do its job better. For example, if nodes David, Dianne and Dakota tell node Ernie the current input image is a picture of Brad Pitt, but node Durango says it is Betty White, and the training program confirms it is Pitt, Ernie will decrease the weight it assigns to Durango's input and increase the weight it gives to that of David, Dianne and Dakota.

In defining the rules and making determinations -- that is, each node decides what to send on to the next tier based on its own inputs from the previous tier -- neural networks use several principles. These include gradient-based training, fuzzy logic, genetic algorithms and Bayesian methods. They may be given some basic rules about object relationships in the space being modeled. For example, a facial recognition system might be instructed, "Eyebrows are found above eyes," or, "Moustaches are below a nose. Moustaches are above and/or beside a mouth." Preloading rules can make training faster and make the model more powerful sooner. But it also builds in assumptions about the nature of the problem space, which may prove to be either irrelevant and unhelpful or incorrect and counterproductive, making the decision about what, if any, rules to build in very important.

3.1.4 Types of Neural Networks

Neural networks are sometimes described in terms of their depth, including how many layers they have between input and output, or the model's so-called hidden layers. This is why the term neural network is used almost synonymously with deep learning. They can also be described by the number of hidden nodes the model has or in terms of how many inputs and outputs each node has. Variations on the classic neural network design allow various forms of forward and backward propagation of information among tiers.

The simplest variant is the feed-forward neural network. This type of artificial neural network algorithm passes information straight through from input to processing nodes to outputs. It may or may not have hidden node layers, making their functioning more interpretable.

More complex are recurrent neural networks. These deep learning algorithms save the output of processing nodes and feed the result back into the model. This is how the model is said to learn.

Convolutional neural networks are popular today, particularly in the realm of image recognition. This specific type of neural network algorithm has been used in many of the most advanced applications of AI including facial recognition, text digitization and natural language processing.

3.2 Convolutional Neural Networks (CNN)

A convolutional neural network (CNN) is a type of artificial neural network used in image recognition and processing that is specifically designed to process pixel data.

CNNs are powerful image processing, artificial intelligence (AI) that use deep learning to perform both generative and descriptive tasks, often using machine vison that includes image and video recognition, along with recommender systems and natural language processing (NLP).

A neural network is a system of hardware and/or software patterned after the operation of neurons in the human brain. Traditional neural networks are not ideal for image processing and must be fed images in reduced-resolution pieces. CNN have their "neurons" arranged more like those of the frontal lobe, the area responsible for processing visual stimuli in humans and other animals. The layers of neurons are arranged in such a way as to cover the entire visual field avoiding the piecemeal image processing problem of traditional neural networks.

A CNN uses a system much like a multilayer perceptron that has been designed for reduced processing requirements. The layers of a CNN consist of an input layer, an output layer and a hidden layer that includes multiple convolutional layers, pooling layers, fully connected layers and normalization layers. The removal of limitations and increase in efficiency for image processing results in a system that is far more effective, simpler to trains limited for image processing and natural language processing.

Chapter 4: Deep Learning

4.1 Introduction

Deep structured learning or hierarchical learning or deep learning in short is part of the family of machine learning methods which are themselves a subset of the broader field of Artificial Intelligence.

Deep learning is a class of machine learning algorithms that use several layers of nonlinear processing units for feature extraction and transformation. Each successive layer uses the output from the previous layer as input.

Deep neural networks, deep belief networks and recurrent neural networks have been applied to fields such as computer vision, speech recognition, natural language processing, audio recognition, social network filtering, machine translation, and bioinformatics where they produced results comparable to and in some cases better than human experts have.

Deep Learning Algorithms and Networks –

- are based on the unsupervised learning of multiple levels of features or representations of the data. Higher-level features are derived from lower level features to form a hierarchical representation.
- use some form of gradient descent for training.

Deep Learning is a subfield of machine learning concerned with algorithms inspired by the structure and function of the brain called artificial neural networks.

If you are just starting out in the field of deep learning or

you had some experience with neural networks some time ago, you may be confused. I know I was confused initially and so were many of my colleagues and friends who learned and used neural networks in the 1990s and early 2000s.

The leaders and experts in the field have ideas of what deep learning is and these specific and nuanced perspectives shed a lot of light on what deep learning is all about.

Deep learning is an aspect of artificial intelligence (AI) that is concerned with emulating the learning approach that human beings use to gain certain types of knowledge. At its simplest, deep learning can be thought of as a way to automate predictive analytics.

While traditional machine learning algorithms are linear, deep learning algorithms are stacked in a hierarchy of increasing complexity and abstraction. To understand deep learning, imagine a toddler whose first word is dog. The toddler learns what a dog is (and is not) by pointing to objects and saying the word dog. The parent says, "Yes, that is a dog," or, "No, that is not a dog." As the toddler continues to point to objects, he becomes more aware of the features that all dogs possess. What the toddler does, without knowing it, is clarify a complex abstraction (the concept of dog) by building a hierarchy in which each level of abstraction is created with knowledge that was gained from the preceding layer of the hierarchy.

4.2 How Deep Learning Works

Computer programs that use deep learning go through much the same process. Each algorithm in the hierarchy applies a nonlinear transformation on its input and uses what it learns to create a statistical model as output. Iterations continue until the output has reached an acceptable level of accuracy. The number of processing layers through which data must pass is what inspired the label deep.

In traditional machine learning, the learning process is supervised and the programmer has to be very, very specific when telling the computer what types of things it should be looking for when deciding if an image contains a dog or does not contain a dog. This is a laborious process called feature extraction and the computer's success rate depends entirely upon the programmer's ability to accurately define a feature set for "dog." The advantage of deep learning is that the program builds the feature set by itself without supervision. Unsupervised learning is not only faster, but it is usually more accurate.

Initially, the computer program might be provided with training data, a set of images for which a human has labeled each image "dog" or "not dog" with meta tags. The program uses the information it receives from the training data to create a feature set for dog and build a predictive model. In this case, the model the computer first creates might predict that anything in an image that has four legs and a tail should be labeled "dog." Of course, the program is not aware of the labels "four legs" or "tail;" it will simply look for patterns of pixels in the digital data. With each iteration, the predictive model the computer creates becomes more complex and more accurate.

Because this process mimics a system of human neurons, deep learning is sometimes referred to as deep neural learning or deep neural networking. Unlike the toddler, who will take weeks or even months to understand the concept of "dog," a computer program that uses deep learning algorithms can be shown a training set and sort through millions of images, accurately identifying which images have dogs in them within a few minutes.

To achieve an acceptable level of accuracy, deep learning programs require access to immense amounts of training data and processing power, neither of which were easily available to programmers until the era of big data and cloud computing. Because deep learning programming is able to create complex statistical models directly from its own iterative output, it is able to create accurate predictive models from large quantities of unlabeled, unstructured data. This is important as the internet of things (IoT) continues to become more pervasive, because most of the data humans and machines create is unstructured and is not labeled.

Use cases today for deep learning include all types of big data analytics applications, especially those focused on natural language processing (NLP), language translation,

43

medical diagnosis, stock market trading signals, network security and image dentification.

4.3 Using Neural Networks

A type of advanced machine learning algorithm, known as neural networks, underpins most deep learning models. Neural networks come in several different forms, including recurrent neural networks, convolutional neural networks, artificial neural networks and feedforward neural networks, and each has their benefit for specific use cases. However, they all function in somewhat similar ways, by feeding data in and letting the model figure out for itself whether it has made the right interpretation or decision about a given data element.

Neural networks involve a trial-and-error process, so they need massive amounts of data to train on. It's no coincidence that neural networks became popular only after most enterprises embraced big data analytics and accumulated large stores of data. Because the model's first few iterations involve somewhat-educated guesses on the contents of image or parts of speech, the data used during the training stage must be labeled so the model can see if its guess was accurate. This means that, though many enterprises that use big data have large amounts of data, unstructured data is less helpful. Unstructured data can be analyzed by a deep learning model once it has been trained and reaches an acceptable level of accuracy, but deep learning models can't train on unstructured data.

4.4 Examples

Because deep learning models process information in ways similar to the human brain, models can be applied to many tasks people do. Deep learning is currently used in most common image recognition tools, NLP processing and speech recognition software. These tools are starting to appear in applications as diverse as self-driving cars and language translation services.

4.4.1 Image Recognition

Image recognition, in the context of machine vision, is the ability of software to identify objects, places, people, writing and actions in images. Computers can use machine vision technologies in combination with a camera and artificial intelligence software to achieve image recognition.

Image recognition is used to perform a large number of machine-based visual tasks, such as labeling the content of images with meta-tags, performing image content search and guiding autonomous robots, self-driving cars and accident avoidance systems.

While human and animal brains recognize objects with ease, computers have difficulty with the task. Software for image recognition requires deep machine learning. Performance is best on convolutional neural net processors as the specific task otherwise requires massive amounts of power for its compute-intensive nature. Image recognition algorithms can function by use of comparative 3D models, appearances from different angles using edge detection or by components. Image recognition algorithms are often trained on millions of pre-labeled pictures with guided computer learning.

Current and future applications of image recognition include smart photo libraries, targeted advertising, the interactivity of media, accessibility for the visually impaired and enhanced research capabilities. Google, Facebook, Microsoft, Apple and Pinterest are among the many companies that are investing significant resources and research into image recognition and related applications. Privacy concerns over image recognition and similar technologies are controversial as these companies can pull a large volume of data from user photos uploaded to their social media platforms.

4.4.2 Facial Recognition

Facial recognition is a category of biometric software that maps an individual's facial features mathematically and stores the data as a faceprint. The software uses deep learning algorithms to compare a live capture or digital image to the stored faceprint in order to verify an individual's identity. High-quality cameras in mobile devices have made facial recognition a viable option for authentication as well as identification. Apple's iPhone X, for example, includes Face ID technology that lets users unlock their phones with a faceprint mapped by the phone's camera. The phone's software, which is designed with 3-D modeling to resist being spoofed by photos or masks, captures and compares over 30,000 variables. As of this writing, Face ID can be used to authenticate purchases with Apple Pay and in the iTunes Store, App Store and iBooks Store. Apple encrypts and stores faceprint data in the cloud, but authentication takes place directly on the device. Developers can use Amazon Recognition, an image analysis service that's part of the Amazon AI suite, to add facial recognition and analysis features to an application. Google provides a similar capability with its Google Cloud Vision API. The technology, which uses machine learning to detect, match and identify faces, is being used in a wide variety of ways, including entertainment and marketing. The Kinect motion gaming system, for example, uses facial recognition to differentiate among players. Smart advertisements in airports are now able to identify the gender, ethnicity and approximate age of a passersby and target the advertisement to the person's demographic. Facebook uses facial recognition software to tag individuals in photographs. Each time an individual is tagged in a photograph, the software stores mapping information about that person's facial characteristics. Once enough data has been collected, the software can use that information to identify a specific individual's face when it appears in a new photograph. To protect people's privacy, a feature called Photo Review notifies the Facebook member who has been identified. Currently, there are no laws in the United States that specifically protect an individual's biometric data. Facial recognition systems are currently being studied or deployed for airport security and it's estimated that more than half the United States population has already had their faceprint captured. According the Department of Homeland Security, the only way to avoid having biometric information collected when traveling internationally is to refrain from traveling. The General Data Protection Regulation (GDPR) for European Member States does address biometric data.

Chapter 5: TensorFlow

5.1 Introduction

TensorFlow is an open source software library created by Google that is used to implement machine learning and deep learning systems. These two names contain a series of powerful algorithms that share a common challenge— to allow a computer to learn how to automatically spot complex patterns and/or to make best possible decisions.

Machine learning is a complex discipline. But implementing machine learning models is far less daunting and difficult than it used to be, thanks to machine learning frameworks—such as Google's TensorFlow—that ease the process of acquiring data, training models, serving predictions, and refining future results.

TensorFlow, at its heart, is a library for dataflow programming. It leverages various optimization techniques to make the calculation of mathematical expressions easier and more performant.

Some of the key features of TensorFlow are:

- Efficiently works with mathematical expressions involving multi-dimensional arrays
- Good support of deep neural networks and machine learning concepts
- GPU/CPU computing where the same code can be executed on both architectures

- High scalability of computation across machines and huge data sets
- Together, these features make TensorFlow the perfect framework for machine intelligence at a production scale.

In this TensorFlow chapter, you will learn how you can use simple yet powerful machine learning methods in TensorFlow and how you can use some of its auxiliary libraries to debug, visualize, and tweak the models created with it.

5.2 How TensorFlow Works

TensorFlow allows developers to create dataflow graphs—structures that describe how data moves through a graph, or a series of processing nodes. Each node in the graph represents a mathematical operation, and each connection or edge between nodes is a multidimensional data array, or tensor.

TensorFlow provides all of this for the programmer by way of the Python language. Python is easy to learn and work with, and provides convenient ways to express how high-level abstractions can be coupled together. Nodes and tensors in TensorFlow are Python objects, and TensorFlow applications are themselves Python applications.

The actual math operations, however, are not performed in Python. The libraries of transformations that are available through TensorFlow are written as high-

51

performance C++ binaries. Python just directs traffic between the pieces, and provides high-level programming abstractions to hook them together.

TensorFlow applications can be run on most any target that's convenient: a local machine, a cluster in the cloud, iOS and Android devices, CPUs or GPUs. If you use Google's own cloud, you can run TensorFlow on Google's custom TensorFlow Processing Unit (TPU) silicon for further acceleration. The resulting models created by TensorFlow, though, can be deployed on most any device where they will be used to serve predictions.

5.3 Installing TensorFlow

We will be using the TensorFlow Python API, which works with Python 2.7 and Python 3.3+. The GPU version (Linux only) requires the Cuda Toolkit 7.0+ and cuDNN v2+.

We shall use the Conda package dependency management system to install TensorFlow. Conda allows us to separate multiple environments on a machine. You can learn how to install Conda from here.

After installing Conda, we can create the environment that we will use for TensorFlow installation and use. The following command will create our environment with some additional libraries like NumPy, which is very useful once we start to use TensorFlow.

The Python version installed inside this environment is 2.7, and we will use this version in this article.

```
conda create --name TensorflowEnv biopython
```

To make things easy, we are installing biopython here instead of just NumPy. This includes NumPy and a few other packages that we will be needing. You can always install the packages as you need them using the conda

install or the pip install commands.

The following command will activate the created Conda environment. We will be able to use packages installed within it, without mixing with packages that are installed globally or in some other environments.

```
source activate TensorFlowEnv
```

The pip installation tool is a standard part of a Conda environment. We will use it to install the TensorFlow library. Prior to doing that, a good first step is updating pip to the latest version, using the following command:

```
pip install --upgrade pip
```

Now we are ready to install TensorFlow, by running:

```
pip install tensorflow
```

The download and build of TensorFlow can take several minutes. At the time of writing, this installs TensorFlow 1.1.0.

5.4 Data Flow Graphs

In TensorFlow, computation is described using data flow graphs. Each node of the graph represents an instance of a mathematical operation (like addition, division, or multiplication) and each edge is a multi-dimensional data set (tensor) on which the operations are performed.

As TensorFlow works with computational graphs, they are managed where each node represents the instantiation of an operation where each operation has zero or more inputs and zero or more outputs.

Edges in TensorFlow can be grouped in two categories: Normal edges transfer data structure (tensors) where it is possible that the output of one operation becomes the input for another operation and special edges, which are used to control dependency between two nodes to set the order of operation where one node waits for another to finish.

5.5 Simple Expressions

Before we move on to discuss elements of TensorFlow, we will first do a session of working with TensorFlow, to get a feeling of what a TensorFlow program looks like.

Let's start with simple expressions and assume that, for some reason, we want to evaluate the function y = 5*x + 13 in TensorFlow fashion.

In simple Python code, it would look like:

```
x = -2.0
```

y = 5*x + 13

print y

which gives us in this case a result of 3.0.

Now we will convert the above expression into TensorFlow terms.

5.6 Constants

In TensorFlow, constants are created using the function constant, which has the signature constant(value, dtype=None, shape=None, name='Const', verify_shape=False) , where value is an actual constant value which will be used in further computation, dtype is the data type parameter (e.g., float32/64, int8/16, etc.), shape is optional dimensions, name is an optional name for the tensor, and the last parameter is a boolean which indicates verification of the shape of values.

If you need constants with specific values inside your training model, then the constant object can be used as in following example:

```
z = tf.constant( 5.2 , name= "x" , dtype=tf.float32)
```

5.7 Variables

Variables in TensorFlow are in-memory buffers containing tensors which have to be explicitly initialized and used in-graph to maintain state across session. By simply calling the constructor the variable is added in computational graph.

Variables are especially useful once you start with training models, and they are used to hold and update parameters. An initial value passed as an argument of a constructor represents a tensor or object which can be converted or returned as a tensor. That means if we want to fill a variable with some predefined or random values to be used afterwards in the training process and updated over iterations, we can define it in the following way:

```
k = tf.Variable(tf.zeros([ 1 ]), name= "k" )
```

Another way to use variables in TensorFlow is in calculations where that variable isn't trainable and can be defined in the following way:

```
k = tf.Variable(tf.add(a, b), trainable= False )
```

5.8 Sessions

In order to actually evaluate the nodes, we must run a computational graph within a session.

A session encapsulates the control and state of the TensorFlow runtime. A session without parameters will use the default graph created in the current session, otherwise the session class accepts a graph parameter, which is used in that session to be executed.

Below is a brief code snippet that shows how the terms defined above can be used in TensorFlow to calculate a simple linear function.

```
import tensorflow as tf

x = tf.constant( -2.0 , name= "x" , dtype=tf.float32)

a = tf.constant( 5.0 , name= "a" , dtype=tf.float32)

b = tf.constant( 13.0 , name= "b" , dtype=tf.float32)


y = tf.Variable(tf.add(tf.multiply(a, x), b))


init = tf.global_variables_initializer()


with tf.Session() as session:

    session.run(init)

     print session.run(y)
```

5.9 Benefits

The single biggest benefit TensorFlow provides for machine learning development is abstraction. Instead of dealing with the nitty-gritty details of implementing algorithms, or figuring out proper ways to hitch the output of one function to the input of another, the developer can focus on the overall logic of the application. TensorFlow takes care of the details behind the scenes.

TensorFlow offers additional conveniences for developers who need to debug and gain introspection into TensorFlow apps. The eager execution mode lets you evaluate and modify each graph operation separately and transparently, instead of constructing the entire graph as a single opaque object and evaluating it all at once. The TensorBoard visualization suite lets you inspect and profile the way graphs run by way of an interactive, web-based dashboard.

And of course, TensorFlow gains many advantages from the backing of an A-list commercial outfit in Google. Google has not only fueled the rapid pace of development behind the project, but created many significant offerings around TensorFlow that make it easier to deploy and easier to use: the above-mentioned TPU silicon for accelerated performance in Google's cloud; an online hub for sharing models created with the framework; in-browser and mobile-friendly incarnations of the framework; and much more.

One caveat: Some details of TensorFlow's implementation make it hard to obtain totally deterministic model-training results for some training jobs. Sometimes a model trained on one system will vary slightly from a model trained on another, even when they are fed the exact same data. The reasons for this are slippery—e.g., how random numbers are seeded and where, or certain non-deterministic behaviors when using GPUs). That said, it is possible to work around those issues, and TensorFlow's team is considering more controls to affect determinism in a workflow.

Chapter 6: Python & R Codes of Machine Learning Algorithms

The idea behind creating this chapter is to simplify the journey of aspiring data scientists and machine learning enthusiasts across the world. Through this guide, I will enable you to work on machine learning problems and gain from experience. I am providing a high-level understanding about various machine learning algorithms along with R & Python codes to run them. These should be sufficient to get your hands dirty.

Broadly, there are 3 types of Machine Learning Algorithms.

6.1 Supervised Learning

How it works: This algorithm consists of a target / outcome variable (or dependent variable) which is to be predicted from a given set of predictors (independent variables). Using these set of variables, we generate a function that map inputs to desired outputs. The training process continues until the model achieves a desired level of accuracy on the training data. Examples of Supervised Learning: Regression, Decision Tree, Random Forest, KNN, Logistic Regression etc.

6.2 Unsupervised Learning

How it works: In this algorithm, we do not have any target or outcome variable to predict / estimate. It is used for clustering population in different groups, which is widely used for segmenting customers in different groups for specific intervention. Examples of Unsupervised Learning: Apriori algorithm, K-means.

6.3 Reinforcement Learning:

How it works: Using this algorithm, the machine is trained to make specific decisions. It works this way: the machine is exposed to an environment where it trains itself continually using trial and error. This machine learns from past experience and tries to capture the best possible knowledge to make accurate business decisions. Example of Reinforcement Learning: Markov Decision Process

6.4 List of Common Machine Learning Algorithms

Here is the list of commonly used machine learning algorithms. These algorithms can be applied to almost any data problem:

- Linear Regression
- Logistic Regression
- Decision Tree
- SVM
- Naive Bayes
- kNN
- K-Means
- Random Forest
- Dimensionality Reduction Algorithms
- Gradient Boosting algorithms

6.5 Linear Regression

It is used to estimate real values (cost of houses, number of calls, total sales etc.) based on continuous variable(s).

Here, we establish relationship between independent and dependent variables by fitting a best line. This best fit line is known as regression line and represented by a linear equation $Y = a * X + b$.

The best way to understand linear regression is to relive this experience of childhood. Let us say, you ask a child in fifth grade to arrange people in his class by increasing order of weight, without asking them their weights! What do you think the child will do? He / she would likely look (visually analyze) at the height and build of people and arrange them using a combination of these visible parameters. This is linear regression in real life! The child has actually figured out that height and build would be correlated to the weight by a relationship, which looks like the equation above.

In this equation:

Y – Dependent Variable

a – Slope

X – Independent variable

b – Intercept

These coefficients a and b are derived based on minimizing the sum of squared difference of distance between data points and regression line.

Python Code:

```
#Import Library

#Import other necessary libraries like pandas,
numpy...

from sklearn import linear_model

#Load Train and Test datasets

#Identify feature and response variable(s) and
values must be numeric and numpy arrays

x_train=input_variables_values_training_datase
ts

y_train=target_variables_values_training_datas
ets

x_test=input_variables_values_test_datasets

# Create linear regression object

linear = linear_model.LinearRegression()

# Train the model using the training sets and
check score

linear.fit(x_train, y_train)

linear.score(x_train, y_train)
```

```
#Equation coefficient and Intercept

print('Coefficient: \n', linear.coef_)

print('Intercept: \n', linear.intercept_)

#Predict Output

predicted= linear.predict(x_test)
```

R Code:

```
#Load Train and Test datasets

#Identify feature and response variable(s) and
values must be numeric and numpy arrays

x_train <- input_variables_values_training_dat
asets

y_train <- target_variables_values_training_da
tasets

x_test <- input_variables_values_test_datasets

x <- cbind(x_train,y_train)

# Train the model using the training sets and
check score

linear <- lm(y_train ~ ., data = x)
```

```
summary(linear)

#Predict Output

predicted= predict(linear,x_test)
```

6.6 Logistics Regression

Don't get confused by its name! It is a classification not a regression algorithm. It is used to estimate discrete values (Binary values like 0/1, yes/no, true/false) based on given set of independent variables(s). In simple words, it predicts the probability of occurrence of an event by fitting data to a logit function. Hence, it is also known as logit regression. Since, it predicts the probability, its output values lie between 0 and 1 (as expected).

Again, let us try and understand this through a simple example.

Let's say your friend gives you a puzzle to solve. There are only 2 outcome scenarios – either you solve it or you don't. Now imagine, that you are being given wide range of puzzles / quizzes in an attempt to understand which subjects you are good at. The outcome to this study would be something like this – if you are given a trigonometry based tenth grade problem, you are 70% likely to solve it. On the other hand, if it is grade fifth history question, the probability of getting an answer is only 30%. This is what Logistic Regression provides you.

Python Code:

```
#Import Library

from sklearn.linear_model import LogisticRegre
ssion

#Assumed you have, X (predictor) and Y (target
) for training data set and x_test(predictor)
of test_dataset

# Create logistic regression object

model = LogisticRegression()

# Train the model using the training sets and
check score

model.fit(X, y)

model.score(X, y)

#Equation coefficient and Intercept

print('Coefficient: \n', model.coef_)

print('Intercept: \n', model.intercept_)

#Predict Output

predicted= model.predict(x_test)
```

R Code:

```
x <- cbind(x_train,y_train)

# Train the model using the training sets and
check score

logistic <- glm(y_train ~ ., data = x,family='
binomial')

summary(logistic)

#Predict Output

predicted= predict(logistic,x_test)
```

6.7 Decision Tree

This is one of my favorite algorithms and I use it quite frequently. It is a type of supervised learning algorithm that is mostly used for classification problems. Surprisingly, it works for both categorical and continuous dependent variables. In this algorithm, we split the population into two or more homogeneous sets. This is done based on most significant attributes/ independent variables to make as distinct groups as possible.

Python Code:

```
#Import Library
```

```
#Import other necessary libraries like pandas,
numpy...

from sklearn import tree

#Assumed you have, X (predictor) and Y (target
) for training data set and x_test(predictor)
of test_dataset

# Create tree object

model = tree.DecisionTreeClassifier(criterion=
'gini') # for classification, here you can cha
nge the algorithm as gini or entropy (informat
ion gain) by default it is gini

# model = tree.DecisionTreeRegressor() for reg
ression

# Train the model using the training sets and
check score

model.fit(X, y)

model.score(X, y)

#Predict Output

predicted= model.predict(x_test)
```

R Code:

```
library(rpart)

x <- cbind(x_train,y_train)

# grow tree

fit <- rpart(y_train ~ ., data = x,method="cla
ss")

summary(fit)

#Predict Output

predicted= predict(fit,x_test)
```

6.8 Support Vector Machine

It is a classification method. In this algorithm, we plot each data item as a point in n-dimensional space (where n is number of features you have) with the value of each feature being the value of a particular coordinate.

For example, if we only had two features like Height and Hair length of an individual, we'd first plot these two variables in two-dimensional space where each point has two co-ordinates (these co-ordinates are known as Support Vectors)

Python Code:

```
#Import Library

from sklearn import svm

#Assumed you have, X (predictor) and Y (target
) for training data set and x_test(predictor)
of test_dataset

# Create SVM classification object

model = svm.svc() # there is various option as
sociated with it, this is simple for classific
ation. You can refer link, for mo# re detail.

# Train the model using the training sets and
check score

model.fit(X, y)

model.score(X, y)

#Predict Output

predicted= model.predict(x_test)
```

R Code:

```
library(e1071)
```

```
x <- cbind(x_train,y_train)

# Fitting model

fit <-svm(y_train ~ ., data = x)

summary(fit)

#Predict Output

predicted= predict(fit,x_test)
```

6.9 Naïve Bayes

It is a classification technique based on Bayes' theorem with an assumption of independence between predictors. In simple terms, a Naive Bayes classifier assumes that the presence of a particular feature in a class is unrelated to the presence of any other feature. For example, a fruit may be considered to be an apple if it is red, round, and about 3 inches in diameter. Even if these features depend on each other or upon the existence of the other features, a naive Bayes classifier would consider all of these properties to independently contribute to the probability that this fruit is an apple.

Naive Bayesian model is easy to build and particularly useful for very large data sets. Along with simplicity, Naive Bayes is known to outperform even highly sophisticated classification methods.

Python Code:

```
#Import Library

from sklearn.naive_bayes import GaussianNB

#Assumed you have, X (predictor) and Y (target
) for training data set and x_test(predictor)
of test_dataset

# Create SVM classification object model = Gau
ssianNB() # there is other distribution for mu
ltinomial classes like Bernoulli Naive Bayes,
Refer link

# Train the model using the training sets and
check score

model.fit(X, y)

#Predict Output

predicted= model.predict(x_test)
```

R Code:

```
library(e1071)

x <- cbind(x_train,y_train)
```

```
# Fitting model

fit <-naiveBayes(y_train ~ ., data = x)

summary(fit)

#Predict Output

predicted= predict(fit,x_test)
```

6.10 KNN

It can be used for both classification and regression problems. However, it is more widely used in classification problems in the industry. K nearest neighbors is a simple algorithm that stores all available cases and classifies new cases by a majority vote of its k neighbors. The case being assigned to the class is most common amongst its K nearest neighbors measured by a distance function.

These distance functions can be Euclidean, Manhattan, Minkowski and Hamming distance. First three functions are used for continuous function and fourth one (Hamming) for categorical variables. If K = 1, then the case is simply assigned to the class of its nearest neighbor. At times, choosing K turns out to be a challenge while performing KNN modeling.

Python Code:

```python
#Import Library

from sklearn.neighbors import KNeighborsClassi
fier

#Assumed you have, X (predictor) and Y (target
) for training data set and x_test(predictor)
of test_dataset

# Create KNeighbors classifier object model

KNeighborsClassifier(n_neighbors=6) # default
value for n_neighbors is 5

# Train the model using the training sets and
check score

model.fit(X, y)

#Predict Output

predicted= model.predict(x_test)
```

R Code:

```r
library(knn)

x <- cbind(x_train,y_train)

# Fitting model
```

```
fit <-knn(y_train ~ ., data = x,k=5)

summary(fit)

#Predict Output

predicted= predict(fit,x_test)
```

6.11 K-Means

It is a type of unsupervised algorithm which solves the clustering problem. Its procedure follows a simple and easy way to classify a given data set through a certain number of clusters (assume k clusters). Data points inside a cluster are homogeneous and heterogeneous to peer groups.

How K-means forms cluster:

K-means picks k number of points for each cluster known as centroids.

Each data point forms a cluster with the closest centroids i.e. k clusters.

Finds the centroid of each cluster based on existing cluster members. Here we have new centroids.

As we have new centroids, repeat step 2 and 3. Find the closest distance for each data point from new centroids and get associated with new k-clusters. Repeat this process until convergence occurs i.e. centroids does not change.

How to determine value of K:

In K-means, we have clusters and each cluster has its own centroid. Sum of square of difference between centroid and the data points within a cluster constitutes within sum of square value for that cluster. Also, when the sum of square values for all the clusters are added, it becomes total within sum of square value for the cluster solution.

We know that as the number of cluster increases, this value keeps on decreasing but if you plot the result you may see that the sum of squared distance decreases sharply up to some value of k, and then much more slowly after that. Here, we can find the optimum number of clusters.

Python Code:

```
#Import Library

from sklearn.cluster import KMeans

#Assumed you have, X (attributes) for training
data set and x_test(attributes) of
test_dataset

# Create KNeighbors classifier object model

k_means = KMeans(n_clusters=3, random_state=0)

# Train the model using the training sets and
check score
```

```
model.fit(X)

#Predict Output

predicted= model.predict(x_test)
```

R Code:

```
library(cluster)

fit <- kmeans(X, 3) # 5 cluster solution
```

6.12 Random Forest

Random Forest is a trademark term for an ensemble of decision trees. In Random Forest, we've collection of decision trees (so known as "Forest"). To classify a new object based on attributes, each tree gives a classification and we say the tree "votes" for that class. The forest chooses the classification having the most votes (over all the trees in the forest).

Each tree is planted & grown as follows:

If the number of cases in the training set is N, then sample of N cases is taken at random but with replacement. This sample will be the training set for growing the tree.

If there are M input variables, a number m<<M is specified such that at each node, m variables are selected at random out of the M and the best split on

these m is used to split the node. The value of m is held constant during the forest growing.

Each tree is grown to the largest extent possible. There is no pruning.

Python Code:

```
#Import Library

from sklearn.ensemble import
RandomForestClassifier

#Assumed you have, X (predictor) and Y
(target) for training data set and
x_test(predictor) of test_dataset

# Create Random Forest object

model= RandomForestClassifier()

# Train the model using the training sets and
check score

model.fit(X, y)

#Predict Output

predicted= model.predict(x_test)
```

R Code:

```
library(randomForest)

x <- cbind(x_train,y_train)

# Fitting model

fit <- randomForest(Species ~ ., x,ntree=500)

summary(fit)

#Predict Output

predicted= predict(fit,x_test)
```

6.13 Dimensionally Reduction Algorithms

In the last 4-5 years, there has been an exponential increase in data capturing at every possible stage. Corporates/ Government Agencies/ Research organizations are not only coming with new sources but also, they are capturing data in great detail.

For example: E-commerce companies are capturing more details about customer like their demographics, web crawling history, what they like or dislike, purchase history, feedback and many others to give them personalized attention more than your nearest grocery shopkeeper.

As a data scientist, the data we are offered also consist of many features, this sounds good for building good robust model but there is a challenge. How'd you identify highly significant variable(s) out 1000 or 2000? In such cases, dimensionality reduction algorithm helps us along with various other algorithms like Decision Tree, Random Forest, PCA, Factor Analysis, identify based on correlation matrix, missing value ratio and others.

Python Code:

```
#Import Library

from sklearn import decomposition

#Assumed you have training and test data set a
s train and test

# Create PCA obeject pca= decomposition.PCA(n_
components=k) #default value of k =min(n_sampl
e, n_features)

# For Factor analysis

#fa= decomposition.FactorAnalysis()

# Reduced the dimension of training dataset us
ing PCA
```

```
train_reduced = pca.fit_transform(train)

#Reduced the dimension of test dataset

test_reduced = pca.transform(test)

#For more detail on this, please refer  this l
ink.
```

R Code:

```
library(stats)

pca <- princomp(train, cor = TRUE)

train_reduced  <- predict(pca,train)

test_reduced  <- predict(pca,test)
```

Chapter 7: Conclusion

7.1 Conclusion

This book is aimed at anyone who wants to learn about those algorithms, whether you're an experienced data scientist or developer looking to parlay existing skills into a new environment.

I aimed first and foremost at making sure that you understand the algorithms, neural networks, deep learning, TensorFlow, pattern recognition, face recognition and codes in python/R. Some of them are fairly tricky and tie into other concepts in statistics and machine learning.

I'd suggest that it's worth doing additional reading around any unfamiliar concept that comes up as you work through this book, as machine learning knowledge tends to tie together synergistically; the more you have, the more readily you'll understand new concepts as you expand your toolkit.

Beyond the transfer of knowledge and practical skills, this book looks to achieve a more important goal; specifically, to discuss and convey some of the qualities that are common to skilled machine learning practitioners. These include creativity, demonstrated both in the definition of sophisticated architectures and problem- specific cleaning techniques. Rigor is another key quality, emphasized throughout this book by a focus on measuring performance against meaningful targets and critically assessing early efforts.

Finally, this book makes no effort to obscure the realities of working on solving data challenges: the mixed results of early trials, large iteration counts, and frequent impasses. Yet at the same time, using a mixture of toy examples, dissection of expert approaches and, toward the end of the book, more real-world challenges, we show how a creative, tenacious, and rigorous approach can break down these barriers and deliver meaningful results.

We hope you have enjoyed learning about "Advanced Machine Learning". Machine learning is a continuously developing field. Because of this, there are some considerations to keep in mind as you work with machine learning methodologies, or analyze the impact of machine learning processes. Machine learning is a continuously developing field. Because of this, there are some considerations to keep in mind as you work with machine learning methodologies, or analyze the impact of machine learning processes.

As you finished the book, I wish you the best of luck and encourage you to enjoy yourself as you go, tackling the content prepared for you and applying what you've learned to new domains or data.

Good Luck!